Grace Campbell is on a constant mission to undermine the patriarchy and poke a finger at those things in life which make women feel rubbish about themselves. She is a critically acclaimed stand-up, law-changing feminist activist, and co-host of the podcast *Football, Feminism + Everything In Between* with her father, Alastair Campbell.

In 2019, after a sell-out run at the Edinburgh Festival of her debut show, 'Why I'm Never Going Into Politics', Grace launched The Disgraceful Club, a stand-up night in Soho for female and LGBTQI+ comedians to celebrate their disgraceful tendencies, own their shame and inspire others to do the same. Grace's first book, *Amazing Disgrace: A Book About "Shame"*, was published by Hodder*Studio* in October 2020. She lives in London.

THE FUTURE OF MEN

Grace Campbell

unbound

First published in 2020

Unbound
Level 1, Devonshire House, One Mayfair Place, London W1J 8AJ
www.unbound.com

With the kind permission of Tortoise Media

Text design by Ellipsis, Glasgow

A CIP record for this book is available from the British Library

ISBN 978-1-80018-011-6 (paperback)
ISBN 978-1-80018-016-1 (ebook)

Printed in Great Britain by CPI Group (UK)

1 3 5 7 9 8 6 4 2

FOREWORD

Where and who do we want to be?

How might we get there?

What might happen if we stay on our current course?

This is one of the five books that, together, comprise the first set of FUTURES essays. Each short book in the set presents a beautifully written, original future vision by an accomplished writer and subject expert. Read individually, we hope these essays will inform, entertain and challenge. Together, we hope they will inspire readers to imagine what might lie ahead, to figure out how they might like the future to look, and think about how, collectively, we might make the transition from here to there, from now to then.

Over the life of the series we aim to publish a diverse range of voices, covering as broad a view of the future as possible. We ask our authors to write in a spirit of pragmatic hope, and with a commitment to map out potential future landscapes, highlighting both beauties and dangers. We are hugely proud of each of the essays individually, and of the set overall. We hope you get as much out of reading – and arguing with – them as we have from the process of getting them out into the world.

This first set of FUTURES would have been impossible to publish without the enthusiastic support of Tortoise Media, Unbound and the subscribers whose names you'll find listed at the back of each essay. Michael Kowalski, Tortoise's Head of Product, introduced co-founder Katie Vanneck-Smith to the idea, and she made it happen. Annabel Shepherd-Barron's unparalleled strategic capabilities kept the project steady and on course. Matthew d'Ancona offered superb editorial guidance with extraordinary kindness and generosity of spirit, and Jon Hill's designs for the book jackets are elegant perfection. Fiona Lensvelt, DeAndra Lupu and their colleagues at Unbound have proved wonderfully creative and flexible throughout.

This first set of FUTURES essays was commissioned in autumn 2019, in the midst of the Brexit saga, and edited in spring 2020, in lockdown, as Covid-19 changed everything. As we write, it looks unlikely that, by the time you read this, our lives will have settled into any kind of normal – old or new. Still, argument, wit and enlightened thought remain amongst our greatest strengths as a species, and even during an era as stressful and disorienting as the one we are experiencing, imagination, hope and compassion can help us mine greater reserves of resilience than we might expect. We hope these essays can, in a small way, help us find some light at the end of the tunnel.

Professor Max Saunders, Series Editor
Dr Lisa Gee, Programme Director and Editor
May 2020

THE FUTURE OF MEN

> 'The natural world is the greatest source of excitement. The greatest source of visual beauty. It is the greatest source of so much in life that makes life worth living.'
>
> – David Attenborough on the world

Aka Grace Campbell on men.

Hey, men – I know what you're thinking! #notallmen but quite a lot of you will be thinking why should you listen to some young female comedian on the future of men? But you've gotta bear with me here because I am a funny feminist, and a serious one, too. And, seriously, we need to talk about feminism. Because feminism can be a big part of your future, men, and women, and everything in between. Promise.

So put to one side any prejudice you might have. Lose your 'stick to comedy' troll if it's in your head. When I was asked by Tortoise to be part of the FUTURES series, there were obvious themes for me. Feminism, sex, comedy: I am very active in all three of those. Wink, wink. Wank. Wank. Wank.

So, it was my choice to write about something I knew a lot of people would say I am ill-equipped to write about. But what David Attenborough says (see page 1) about the natural world really sums up the way I feel about men, and why I feel qualified to write about their future. To me men are the greatest source of excitement. The greatest source of visual beauty. They are the greatest source of so much in life that makes life worth living. I wanted to write about the thing that I have been observing my whole life: men.

Men are my wildlife. They always have been. For as long as I can remember, I have been observing men in the way David Attenborough observes animals. I watch men in the wild (pubs and football matches) with Attenborough's eager and fascinated voice in my head helping me describe how every intricate movement of a man has another, much deeper, much more profound meaning to the way of life.

I talk about men a lot in my work. When we did poetry at school, muses were always women, and I knew we were missing a trick there. I realised that women have been making muses of men for a long time, just without deserved credit. I decided I would have men as my muse. In my stand-up comedy I make jokes about my dad, my boyfriend, Boris Johnson, Mick Hucknall and Jeremy Corbyn, to name a few.

I have a certain amount of sympathy for men because I feel that, right now, a great many men are confused about their place in society. Never has there been a time where the idea of 'being a man' has been so dubious. The modern man is stuck halfway between the pressures of traditional masculinity and the liberation of feminism. They're puppies having to choose between their new owners and their real parents, sitting gormlessly on the floor, with no idea who to choose. Unfortunately, men aren't as easy to train as puppies, but I hope this essay will change that.

Jokes aside, this conflict in masculinity is all happening despite men still seeming to have most of the power. If by power we mean senior positions in politics, business, the courts, and pretty much all big institutions. Men are in charge of too many of those. Men also take up most of the negative space in the UK. Murderers, rapists, trolls and owners of bad personal hygiene are statistically more likely to be men. Truly, men are 81 per cent more likely to have bad breath than anyone else, according to a mental survey I did of all of my ex-lovers.

I've been a feminist since I was pretty young. At the age of seven I cut the hair off my Barbie dolls because I disagreed with the designers who were trying to tell us that all women should have long blonde hair and big tits. At seventeen, when I did have blonde hair and humungous tits, I worked on the No More Page 3 campaign, to get rid of titty pics from the third page of the *Sun*. I knew then and now that there is nothing wrong with a titty pic; I have a painting of my boobs hanging up on my bedroom wall, that's how much I appreciate my tits. However, I did think that on the third page of a family paper this was not on.

In my early twenties I co-founded a feminist group called the Pink Protest; we worked on the #freeperiods campaign, to end period poverty in the UK. If you don't know what period poverty is, that's fine. I didn't know a huge amount either, having grown up in a privileged household where essentials like that were just always there. My mum still bought me tampons after she started the menopause, so then there were double tampons for me!

But we should all know about it, and there is no comedy in this – one in ten girls who bleed in the UK can't afford menstrual products when they're on their period, meaning they have to use tissue or socks to soak up their period blood. This is Britain, in 2020! Sometimes these kids' lack of menstrual care means they have to miss out on school and lose out on their education. Our campaign has had some success and now the government has promised to end period poverty in all schools and universities in the United Kingdom. But we need always to put pressure on our governments to be doing better on issues like this.

That was heavy. Back to comedy... At twenty-one, I made a feminist prank show for Channel 4 called *Riot Girls*. In *Riot Girls*, I worked with some other extremely funny women and we pranked members of the public – men and women – on gender issues. We covered things that we, as young women, were particularly ticked off about. For example, we did one about men and their reluctance to use contraception.

This is something that has always ticked me off, this whole fact that women have to worry about contraception when men (like Boris Johnson) can just cum wherever they choose and not have to think about the consequences!

I actually once invoiced a boy because he came in me without my permission. Yes, lads, you have to ask a woman's permission before you drop your sperms off at the door of her womb, knock her up and potentially change her life forever. I'd had to pay £30 for an emergency contraception just because some boy with a tie-dye t-shirt and terrible body odour (note, survey), came in me 'by accident'. He never paid me the money, but I'm glad I did the admin anyway.

In this *Riot Girls* sketch we asked men at a university campus if they would take a daily pill as a form of contraception. They all said no and so then I told them that I could hypnotise their dicks to make them temporarily infertile, and they believed me, and they let me do a hypnosis on their (clothed) genitals.

Riot Girls was really fun to make; we got some great reviews. It trended on Twitter because, as expected, people had a lot of opinions on it. Half the viewers loved it for its bawdiness, and the other half, aka men and women who uphold the patriarchy, felt completely attacked. Men, as I've come to learn, are very sensitive in feeling that women are attacking them. Women, on the other hand, have been told by men that we are shit drivers, engineers, football players, politicians and mothers for as long as we've all been here. We still fight back, but it takes a lot more than a comedy sketch to upset us.

I guess that me explaining my feminist calendar of life is just a way of showing you where I'm coming from when writing this essay. If you're reading this, it means that something about this essay has grabbed your attention. It means that, despite me being a woman, you are interested in hearing what I have to say about men. Now, I am not an expert on men. I don't have letters before or after my name. I'm not a psychologist, a relationships expert, or a university lecturer.

I'm a twenty-five-year-old comedian who likes to make jokes about wanking and can often be found in north London pubs having drunken arguments with strangers about the state of the Labour Party.

All the same, my lived experience makes me as much an expert on men as anybody. I was raised around men. I've been in relationships with men. I work with men. I've had sex with men. I hope one day to have sex and make a mini man in my stomach, and then raise him to be an incredible, cool, feminist man, or woman; or whatever they decide to be.

When I first took up the feminist fight, I thought there was no place for men, because they are the ones who have failed to deliver, or even believe in, true equality. But then I began to see and understand how we can't achieve true equality without them, and that there is space for them in this conversation.

And let's face it: whether or not I write this essay, men will always have a future. As long as the world continues to function – which, granted, may not be for much longer – men will be here. What I am hoping to clarify here is what their future could look like if they embraced feminism.

I hope you enjoy my efforts to bring us more together. If you don't, I'm sure you won't hesitate to tell me so online. Or you can come to one of my shows and heckle me. Ninety-five per cent of my hecklers are men with small penises. I made that fact up, too. I've never seen their dicks.

NOT ALL MEN

So before we properly get started, I would just like to clear something up. I love a lot of men. My boyfriend is a man. My dad is a man. Some of my best friends are men. They're all really cool men who I actually choose to spend my time with!

Even more, some of the comedians who have inspired me the most are men. Jack Whitehall, Dave Chappelle, James Acaster, Chris Rock and Will Ferrell are all men I have looked up to and been inspired by.

I think the world is full of talented, innovative, caring and generous men. When we talk about the greatness in humanity, we acknowledge men's part. Sure, a lot of them are letting their side down at the moment: Donald Trump, Boris Johnson, Kim Jong-un and Vladimir Putin, for example, although I plan on keeping mention of those Cabbage Patch dolls to a minimum in this essay.

But men have not been 'cancelled' by women. We just need them to do better. They need it, too. I feel it's important for me to explain this love I have for men near the top of this essay. I want you to know that when I'm talking about men in this book, I mean not all men. I'm sure you're familiar with the phrase 'not all men'. It is commonly employed on the Internet and was originally used as a general defence of men, when a man felt they were on the receiving end of gendered criticisms of their behaviour. I'll give you a good example of a time I heard 'not all men' in action.

Me: Today a man on the Tube tried to put his hand up my skirt.

Female friend: Men are fucking disgusting.

Male friend: No! I wouldn't do that!

Female friend: I know, I wasn't saying you'd do that. I was saying that men who do that are parasites.

Male friend: Not all men are like that, you know??

Of course, when that man touched my bum on the Central Line (ofc it was the Central Line, the only line where the devil shines), I knew that not all men in the world would do that. If I thought all men were going to grope my arse every time I used public transport, I'd never leave the house. I'd rely heavily on Deliveroo and the goodwill of my neighbours. I'd get a dog or a wolf to go out and forage my food for me. I'd only venture outside when England were playing a football match and I would know the streets were safe. I would hide away for four years and then when the World Cup came around I would walk around the streets naked, get on the Tube, and I'd celebrate living in a world where there were no men who might try and pinch my bum.

I know not all men are like that. But, unfortunately, too many are. Too many men still do grope women on public transport(s), or – worse – assault, rape and abuse them. A 2017 survey – a real one, not one of my made-up ones – found that more than half of British women had experienced sexual harassment in the workplace; in the same year, research was published showing that 20 per cent of women, from the age of sixteen, had been the victim of sexual assault. According to the Office of National Statistics, 7.9 per cent of British women suffered domestic abuse during 2018. So, yes, I agree it is not all men, but men have to accept there are far too many of them who think this behaviour is acceptable. This is why this conversation needs to be loud and consistent.

I am an optimistic feminist, so to me the mooncup is half full. If you are a man reading this, I'm going to believe you are a good person. I'm not saying you're perfect; I'm sure you've done things in your life that are questionable. I'm sure you know that better than I do. Whether in relationships, or at work, or the way you've spoken to your mum at times; maybe you once picked your nose and wiped it on your friend's sofa. Nobody is perfect, not even you (yes, you).

Don't get uncomfortable; I'm not perfect either. I've done the snot thing, more times than I'd ever want you to know.

What I'm trying to say is, when I speak about men in this book, you don't need to take offence on behalf of all men. Just take in what I'm saying and think about the other men in your life who might benefit from hearing these things too.

Let's spread this essay like an STD at freshers' week.

DO WE STILL, REALLY, NEED FEMINISM?

I cannot tell you how many times I have been told to 'stop banging on about feminism'. Usually by men who have never let anyone bang on about anything other than why Arsenal don't deserve to win the league this season. There are people who think feminism has done what it needed to do and we don't need it anymore.

There are people who look around and see a world where women have just as much power as men. Women are everywhere, goddammit! They're on TV! They're in films! They're singing songs! They're not only reading the weather but now they're presenting ACTUAL NEWS. They're running countries! They're not only playing football, but also they are commentating on football... on *men's* football! That would probably explain why Roy Keane looks so angry on the telly all the time.

There are people who look at all of that and think that women have finally got all the representation and power they deserve. Feminism defined simply is political, economic and social equality between genders. And if we're using that definition then feminism still has a long way to go. Think of it like the halfway mark at a marathon.

Take the gender pay gap. In the UK, white women earn 18.4 per cent less than men for exactly the same work. This drops to 24 per cent less for black women and 26 per cent less for women of Pakistani or Bangladeshi heritage. Gender and race are preventing women from earning the money they deserve for the work they do. Until that fight is won, we need feminism.

Only 34 per cent of MPs in the House of Commons are women. A paltry 7 per cent of CEOs of FTSE 100 companies are women. Women do 60 per cent more housework than men, a stat which hasn't changed since 2016. Fewer than 20 per cent of the world's landowners are women.

There are fifteen countries where a husband is still allowed to ban his wife from working. Internationally, 50 per cent of all sexual assaults are perpetrated against girls fifteen or younger. At least 200 million girls and women worldwide have undergone female genital mutilation (FGM).

Sorry for bombarding you with facts, but those are just a few of the available percentages and numbers to a) show you

I don't just make up facts, I also find them, and b) prove that feminism is still desperately needed. If you look around you and see a world which represents all genders equally then you need to go get your eyes tested! Specsavers could make a lot of money from you guys.

The challenge of gender equality is also nuanced, to an extent that some feminists would rather not admit. A lot of white women are a huge problem when it comes to feminism – because white feminists have historically only seen their own oppressions as the subject of the fight. When it comes to other people, they often stop. This is why we need intersectional feminism; which means looking further than the people on your road, or the people in your office. Intersectional feminism means not stopping until all women – LGBTQI+ people, women of colour, disabled women – are freed from the oppressions caused by the patriarchy.

But I have some news! There is another group that can be freed if feminism breaks down the patriarchy – drum roll... men!

The patriarchy, in case you didn't know, is the social system which holds men in power when it comes to politics, family, society and property. In this essay, I will mention the patriarchy nearly as much as I manage to slip in the word wank. All in all, it might seem that men are getting a pretty sweet ride on the patriarchy boat. But it's really not all golf clubs and football matches for them.

To make this chat easier, I'm gonna give the patriarchy a nickname. If we were going to give the patriarchy a name, I think we'd call it Pat, right? For short? Pat? Simple? Pat. Bear with me here, I'm sort of making a point. Maybe.

So Pat is a gender-neutral name. Right? You can have Nanny Pat or Grandad Pat, or Postperson Pat. Pat could be a man, or a woman, or non-binary. Meaning, I suppose, that Pat is something that affects all people. Granted Pat discriminates against women the most – I think we've established that – but Pat does affect men, too. Is this the biggest load of bullshit I've ever written in my life? Possibly. And by the way, sorry to anyone who is called Pat – #notallPats, etc.

What is true is that men are affected by the structure of the patriarchy. The patriarchy places all kinds of toxic pressures on men. To be the providers for their families, to be tough, to never show weakness. Men are deprived of the opportunity to be vulnerable. Men can't express themselves freely. Men still have to pretend that they enjoy wearing the uniform of a business suit, that they enjoy smoking cigars and that they like drinking pints even if it makes them fart!

TALKING TO MEN

Caitlin Moran is deservedly one of the most celebrated feminists in the UK. She is also the writer who really helped me get my head around the myriad things that women are conditioned to think they have to do to be seen as appropriately attractive.

On 18 October 2018, Moran tweeted something which got a lot of attention from men: 'Men. Men of Twitter. What are the downsides of being a man? We discuss the downsides of being a woman very frequently – but what's going on with you lovely guys?'

The response to Moran's empathetic tweet was thousands of messages from men expressing their anxieties around being a man today.

One man who, if his profile picture was authentic, looked like he was in his sixties, said: 'Hey thanks for thinking of me. I appreciate the acknowledgment. I worry about losing my job and letting my family down. I could have taken the easy safe path, but I chose to go after something more. If I fail my family suffers. I worry about it daily.'

Another man, who looked a bit younger, said: 'No one will ever buy me flowers. I like flowers.'

Another man, 'Men aren't conditioned to talk to each other about our lives. We meet up, have a four-hour conversation about who would win in a fight between Inspector Gadget and RoboCop, but never get our worries off our chests.'

Trawling through these tweets made me feel sad for these men who appeared to be conscious of the damage that Pat was doing to them, but who didn't quite know how to fix it. I realised in a world where men are the prime cause of problems, we forget that they, and by they I mean the good ones, would appreciate help, too.

Men don't feel there's a space online for them to talk about this stuff without finding themselves boxed into incel communities. Incels, for those who don't know, are 'involuntary celibates': men who identify as members of a subculture based on their inability to find a romantic or sexual partner. Some of them talk nonsense about the 'redistribution of sex'. And really it's no wonder they can't get laid when they talk about sex like it's income tax.

But not all men who want to speak up about gender are anything like this, and those men don't really have a community where they can find civilised debate and a sense of welcome. It's either incel groups or mental health support groups, when perhaps most of them want something in the middle.

While, of course, it isn't the responsibility of feminists to fix this problem, I do think we could be doing more to advance the conversation with men. When we live, work and raise men, I think we need to break down the conversational gap between the genders in the way that Moran did so brilliantly.

So why don't we make this a thing? If you're reading this, why don't you do this with a man in your life. Any man! Your partner, son, boyfriend, father, or even shopkeeper. Ask them: What keeps them up at night? What are the things they feel afraid to say out loud because of Pat? If we can keep having these sometimes uncomfortable conversations with men, this split might fade, and we will be better at understanding the internal problems men face, and they can realise that there is so much power in being vulnerable.

TOO MUCH IS NEVER ENOUGH

But... if women are to compromise and invite men to be part of the feminist conversation, men have to step the feminist fuck up.

A 2019 study (by Ipsos MORI, in collaboration with the Global Institute for Women's Leadership at King's College London – that's a really long title so I definitely haven't made it up) found that three in five men in Britain feel that gender equality won't be achieved unless they also take action to support women's rights.

Which makes me wonder: if three in five men feel that equality can only be done in collaboration with them – where are they? Because I'm not seeing enough of them on the frontline. I'm not hearing enough of them backing women up in disputes on misogyny and sexism.

In my life, I would say less than one in five men I know are personally trying to help gender equality. When I was at school, it was minus one in five boys who wanted girls to be equal to them.

In my late teens, I was dumped by a man who told me that my sense of ambition was 'unattractive' and meant that he 'couldn't imagine a future' with me. I often think about this experience, and how confused I was to find out that someone I liked was a moron.

He was trying to make me feel that something about me I thought was great in fact made me ugly. Like having a wart on my nose or something. I actually did have a wart on my nose a few years before, but, no, it was the fact that I said I wanted to win a BAFTA that made me ugly. But the truth is, this boy didn't like the fact that I had ambition and a strong sense of self because it made him feel smaller.

Too often in my life, men have made me feel like my confidence is a flaw. I'm 'too much', I've been told countless times. As though too much of anything is ever a bad thing.

The most amusing and offensive review that I've ever had written about my comedy was this: 'There's something distasteful about someone demanding attention simply because they can' (*Fest Mag*).

This really made me laugh. Firstly because... I am a stand-up comedian. And breaking news... all comedians are speaking simply because they can. It's literally what standing up on a stage and speaking into a microphone involves. Secondly, I have tried, and struggled, to find a quote like this about a man. Men speaking because they can isn't distasteful, it's just the complete norm. Men speak because they can all the time.

But women are constantly made to feel smaller when they take up too much space. When they have opinions. When they talk louder than the men. Do you know why? Because we're all conditioned to accept these characteristics in men, but not women. I don't hate men for this, but this has got to change. Starting now.

I DON'T HAVE DADDY ISSUES; I HAVE A FATHER WITH ISSUES

This feels like a good moment to start talking about my dad. When it comes to 'being a man' my dad is an anomaly.

You may have heard of my dad. His name is Alastair Campbell. Not to be confused with the guy from UB40 – no, that is Ali Campbell. My dad's the one from politics, though he thinks he can sing and does play the bagpipes, obsessively and rather well. He is the one who worked for Tony Blair and the Labour Party for a very long time.

When I was growing up, in many ways I guess my dad represented what manliness looked like. He was confident, tough, always took up space in a room. He always got people to listen to him. This was something I would watch and admire, and I aspired to achieve myself. Growing up, I wanted to be just like my dad.

My dad didn't come from a powerful or wealthy family. But he had a strong sense of ambition from a very young age. This led to him getting into Cambridge University – which was a big deal for his school and his family. He then met my mum, Fiona Millar, on a graduate training journalism scheme in Devon, and they've been together ever since.

Around the time I was born in 1994, my dad had just started working for Tony Blair, then leader of the Labour Party. He played a key role in helping to get the Labour Party into power (and keep it there) in the elections of 1997, 2001 and 2005. At the heart of political life, he became almost the poster boy for the hyper-masculine, suit-wearing tough-talking spin doctor. His sweary Westminster persona partly inspired the fictional Malcolm Tucker in *The Thick of It*.

So my dad was and is very masculine. But he counteracts that beautifully with the way that he's openly displayed his vulnerabilities to the public as part of his campaign to get us all talking openly about mental health. Since before I blessed his life with my presence, he's had all sorts of issues with mental health. He had an alcohol-induced psychotic breakdown in the eighties, and was then diagnosed with depression and forced to face the dark music in his mind.

He went on medication and later became addicted to exercise – which is a real trend in my family. We are all very fit and very crazy, apart from my mum; she's just very fit and, thankfully, very sane. Since his breakdown, my dad has suffered repeated bouts of depression. This meant I grew up with a dad who was tough and confident outside the house – but at home would sometimes just be lying in the dark, unable to move or speak.

After he left Downing Street, he had a massive crash and decided to write and talk and campaign about mental health. I have a lot of respect for my dad for not trying to hide these problems from the world. Especially at this time, when it was certainly not popular to do so. And it was all the stronger coming from Alastair Campbell, a man who, whatever people's opinions of him, was universally seen as strong, often described as the ultimate alpha male.

For centuries men have been taught to act tough at all times, even when they are struggling. Man up. Don't cry. Stiff upper lip. Men don't feel they can cry at funerals of people close to them. When we still raise boys to think they have to be tough, is it any wonder suicide is still the number one killer for men under forty-five? Too often they don't feel they can talk about their mental health and resort to much more extreme measures.

In the work that my dad has done on mental health, and encouraging men to be more open about theirs, I'd say he's been an incredible campaigner and a feminist. Virtually every week I'll meet someone who tells me that, without my dad's openness, they, or their brother, father, partner, wouldn't have felt confident to 'come out' about their struggles. For this – as well as for raising such an incredible daughter (that's me, I'm the only daughter) – I am incredibly proud of my dad.

FEMINIST IN THEORY, BUT NOT IN PRACTICE

So he is a feminist in theory. He gets it, intellectually, emotionally, spiritually, but practically... OMG...

Our family dog Skye does more around the house than my dad, because at least she hoovers up the crumbs. My dad wouldn't know where the hoover is and he'd probably purposefully break it if he found it, so that he would then have an excuse never to use it again. He'll say the hoover tried to fight him and now there's too much animosity for them to have a positive, functioning relationship.

He uses the word 'can't' instead of 'won't'. He can't change a battery. He can't work the coffee machine. It's an age-old trick, which I think people, aka my mum, fell for in the past.

Oh, and my dad and cooking... well. When he's been asked to go on *Celebrity MasterChef* I've tried to persuade him to do it so the whole country can see how much of a culinary failure he is. In my life I've seen him make one meal! This became a huge event in our calendar, the day Dad made a meal. We'd never thought this would be possible. You know what he did? He heated up a tin of soup (Campbell's, perhaps) in a saucepan, he put bread in the toaster and he bragged for days about the fact that he had 'made soup'!

My mum, who also worked in politics alongside my dad, is a domestic queen. She knows how to do things that I hope never to be able to do. Like drill a hole! She fixes leaks! She cooks like Linda McCartney and she handles the finances like

Kris Jenner. She also looks like Kirsten Cohen from *The O.C.*! What a boss.

When I was a small child, my mum had two full-time jobs. She'd get us ready for school, go to work, come home, cook us dinner, clean up, get us ready for the next day. Of course she had help – we'd have got nowhere as children without our grannies and our nannies, and I'm not gonna lie about that. By the way, I have never used the word granny to describe my grandmas but you have to understand I have compromised for the rhythm of this essay.

My parents were lucky to be able to afford extra help, and we were lucky to have that. Apart from that one nanny, Amanda, who was a Jehovah's Witness and a conspiracy theorist (not saying those two things are linked), and who filled my head with superstitions around death.

But it was still my mum who would do everything when she was at home and not working. Before I was born my parents decided that, as my dad's career was really taking off, this would be the compromise. To a certain degree this makes sense. But the division of labour between my parents has stayed as it was then right up to today, despite the fact that neither of them is working full-time in Westminster (as much as they wish they were, just because it'd mean that twat we currently have wouldn't be there).

In my family home, my mum cooking and cleaning has always been background noise that we are used to thinking is the norm. It wasn't until I became very impassioned with feminism that I realised this was all a farce. I started labelling my parents as theoretical feminists: people who believe in feminism, but don't always practise it in the home. I have become obsessive with telling him off for doing nothing, and telling her off for letting him get away with it. Written down that makes me sound like a really irritating house guest but... their fault now mine.

Truth to tell, the set-up in the Campbell/Millar household isn't unusual in this country. On average in the UK, women devote ten more hours to housework than men. Can you imagine what you could do with ten extra hours a week? You could write a book like this! You could wank a lot. Ten hours a week is training for a marathon (YUCK) or a whole series of *You* on Netflix (HEAVEN).

And more housework means less time to develop a career. Among mothers working part-time, almost a third (30 per cent) said they would increase their hours of employment if there were no barriers to them doing so. But the problem is this: when women become mothers, it is expected of them to put their careers on the backseat for at least the first three years of their child's life, while the father, or in LGBTQI+

couples the breadwinner, can more likely pick what they want to do when it comes to working and parenting a child.

In an especially depressing twist, a study conducted by Montclair State University in the United States found that in heterosexual couples where the woman is the main breadwinner in a family, the more the woman earns means the less likely her partner will contribute to the housework. Yes, you read that correctly. The more a woman earns, the less likely the man is to help around the house...

And I can believe this because, as I know too well, men feel emasculated by their partners if they are higher achieving, higher earners and more powerful. But for women like my mum, they are more willing to accept that that's just how it is, and that they can't fight over who earns more, even though they have just as much potential to earn as much and be as successful.

Housework and childcare are two fundamental aspects of gender equality. Women go on the mummy track and this sets them back while their partners get set forward. Then they start working part-time but it's harder for part-time workers to move up the ladder in companies, and so it is less likely that they will earn a salary to compete with their bread-winning partner.

How can this change?

Well, firstly there's a policy battle to be won, of course. In the UK there was a shared parental leave (SPL) policy, introduced in 2015, that allowed eligible parents to split maternity leave. However, at present, only 2 per cent of men take this. That's two out of a hundred men who want to take paid leave when their child is born!

Now, of course, splitting the leave in most situations isn't enough. Legally all men are entitled to two weeks' paternity leave, paid at minimum statutory rate, compared to the fifty-two weeks to which new mothers are entitled. But what makes this worse is that, according to HMRC data analysed in 2019, less than a third of men take even this brief paternity leave which the law allows them.

This begins a cycle in which women do the lion's share of not only the early childcare, but also the housework! And – because the man is by then (by definition) the breadwinner – the pattern of the woman looking after the child means they struggle to combine these responsibilities at home with the resumption of their professional ambitions.

There is something culturally askew in all this. Shouldn't we reward women for the epic enterprise so many of them display, combining – in effect – full-time employment with full-time parenthood? To call this 'juggling' doesn't do justice to its heroism. We should put women (or men, or anyone else, for that matter) who pull off this feat on a high pedestal. But we don't. We congratulate men for doing just the littlest of things around the house when a woman could be doing that, more and working full-time, and it's what we expect of them.

I often think about a tweet which went viral in 2019. It was from a woman who was a mother and a wife. She had posted a sticker chart that she'd made for her husband. The chart had various household tasks, like washing the dishes, putting the toilet seat down, changing nappies, bathing the kids and cleaning up sick. Each of these tasks had its own specific reward for when the husband managed to complete it six times. The rewards varied depending on the task. From 'No nagging for a week' to 'Naked hula dance from yours truly'. But the one that blew my mind the most was that the man would get a blowjob if he cleaned up his own children's vomit.

Now obviously the Internet is full of fake news and people trying so hard to go viral just for the dopamine hit, so I really can't be sure that the source of this tweet was totally credible. But the fact that I do believe this is a real couple proves my point that we still praise men for doing things that women have been doing forever, with blowjobs and naked hula dancing.

A feature of progress should be that we no longer have to award a man a medal if he has the awesome strength of character and empathy to take his child to the playground or the shops. But even I do this. I gush when I see a man pushing a buggy. 'He must be a great guy!' I exclaim to my friends. Only great guys push buggies!

We are all part of this problem. But, basically, men: you need to accept that housework is not an exclusively female occupation. You need to stop expecting a parade every time you hoover the living room. You need to create the space for women to return to work as fully committed and welcomed employees. You need to ask for flexible work, too, because once men ask for flexible work it will become normalised in companies, and it would become compatible with management and leadership roles and then businesses would embrace it.

And bosses: you need to create a workplace culture where flexible working is not seen in gendered terms as a concession to motherhood, a weakness when sought by men. Your workforce is changing, and, if you want to hire (and keep) the best people, you should change with it.

MAKING MY DAD A FEMINIST

My dad is sixty-two, and sometimes I imagine him waking up one day and deciding that, actually, DIY and gardening are the big passions he never knew he had. He'd go on Amazon (for the first time) and buy loads of tools and toys to embrace his new hobbies.

But then I remember that in no reality would that ever happen. Once my mum asked my dad to mow the lawn, to which he replied, 'If I had wanted to mow lawns, I would have become a gardener.'

Yet he has changed in other ways and, over the years, my relationship with my dad has taught me that men can be feminists. Men can be works-in-progress. My dad had never massively identified as a feminist when he was in Downing Street. But now we co-present a podcast: *Football, Feminism & Everything in Between*! I produce the podcast, which I love because technically it makes me his 'employer'!

The title reflects our respective passions, but it also grew out of long-running arguments between the two of us – often symptomatic of the generational divide between us. It struck us as interesting that football (his great interest) and feminism (mine) are never discussed in the same context. We wanted to see what would happen if we gave it a try.

The immediate inspiration for the podcast was a conversation we had when he was hosting an LBC radio show about feminism – and I phoned in. I thought it was laughable that a man whom I'd witnessed doing nothing about the house was presenting such a show. How dare he! I called in, to his surprise, and outed him – revealing very publicly all of the reasons why he isn't a proper feminist.

This exchange went viral. It was also very well covered in the press. I received hundreds of messages from young women saying that they'd had exactly the same arguments with their own fathers: explaining to men of an older generation why they can't use words like 'birds', or why their laziness around the house has a knock-on effect upon their partners' freedoms and upon their kids' ideals of gender. This is, it turned out, a universal conversation that people my age are having with their fathers.

On our podcast we interview all kinds of people. What I have really enjoyed about it is the opportunity I've had to interview people who I wouldn't have otherwise spoken to because I rarely leave the feminist bubble.

Brian Cox, the actor who has recently taken the world by storm as *Succession*'s media mogul Logan Roy, told us that he's always had a really strong sense of the feminine. Having been raised, in the 1950s and 1960s, by women, and around the Catholic Church, he says he always had an appreciation and understanding of the female experience. It was interesting to hear how this impacted his relationship with feminism; he identified strongly as a feminist.

Some of the podcast episodes have brought around uncomfortable conversations. Conversations that, had I not done the podcast with my dad, with the theme of football, I may never have had. Jamie Carragher, ex-Liverpool player and football pundit, was definitely shocked when I asked him if he talks to his teenage daughter about periods. 'NO!' he said. 'Never done that.' But then when my dad explained to him that me talking about periods has normalised them for him, Carragher seemed to listen, and who knows, maybe the Carragher household now has an open conversation on the menstrual cycle!

We did one episode with Sean Dyche, the manager of Burnley FC, of which my dad is a lifelong fan. Dyche had a lot to say on feminism and football. One thing which really enlightened me was that there is currently a pressure in football for a player to come out as gay. FIFA and the FA are desperate for someone to come out to prove that there isn't institutional homophobia in football, but Dyche said that probably players are reluctant to do this because they will then become the poster boy for gay footballers.

Having conversations with famous footballers like Carragher, Dyche and Joey Barton made me realise how important it is to talk to men because, ultimately, they're very simple beings and their opinions are actually very easy to change.

For this book, I have talked to the three most important men in my life about the future of men. First up is the man who took part in the creation of me, along with my mum. My parents have only had sex three times and one of them was to make me.

DAD (ALASTAIR)

Grace (G):   Dad, can a man be a feminist?

Alastair (A): Yes. You made me realise this really, by all of the conversations we've had. You've argued that men need to be feminists since you were young.

G: So why aren't men taking that much action to help gender equality?

A: I think a lot of men, historically, have seen the idea of equality as a threat, and that if there is to be equality between men and women that can't be delivered by women coming up, it has to be delivered by men going down. You can see how they think that, but I think if you said to most men who are parents today, 'Do you think your daughter should have exactly the same chances as your son?' they'll say: 'Yes.' But in terms of what they practise outside of the house, it probably wouldn't parallel that. You'd think after two women prime ministers, and having the Queen as such a strong woman... but still with those two examples, the norm is to see the man as a powerful figure.

G: Define 'toxic masculinity'.

A: When maleness becomes offensive and brutish. You see it a lot at football. You see it in the media.

G: Growing up, where did your ambition come from?

A: My dad was ambitious on one level, as a vet, but he didn't want to change the world. I don't know where mine came from. I always felt I had to do something special and a bit different. I didn't know what it was going to be. I'd have liked to have been, like, Cristiano Ronaldo-level of football.

G: Well, you didn't have the talent.

A: No, but I have played with Maradona.

Note: My dad speaks about the time he played football with Maradona once a day. No joke, it is a rule he has. The game was thirteen years ago.

G: Knew you'd try and get this in. Did your mum teach you to do the housework?

A: No. We did washing up and that stuff. My mum saw herself as the kind of 'doer'. My dad did loads. He built extensions on the house.

G: Mmmm... do you do that?

A: No, I wouldn't know where to start.

G: Why don't you do anything around the house?

A: I think it's a mix of... I've never liked doing what I define as 'drudge stuff'.

G: But you don't mind other people doing it?

A: Don't mind it. No.

G: So you don't watch Mum [Fiona] doing all of the 'drudge stuff', and think: 'Oh, I'd like to spare her that twenty minutes she's about to spend doing that, while I sit on the sofa.'

A: I don't always sit on the sofa, sometimes I sit on the chair... No, I can't say I'm proud of it.

Interesting that he's not proud of it and yet hasn't tried to do anything about it.

G: But you've never tried to change it so clearly it doesn't bother you that much.

A: For example, I can load the dishwasher, but I don't know how to work it.

G: But it's the simplest thing in the world.

A: Maybe, but I can't do it.

G: But you can do it.

A: The one time your mum tried to show me how to use the coffee machine, I virtually broke the thing.

G: I'm sure you battered it on purpose so that you'd never have to do it again. Why do you think it's always women who do this work?

A: Because of the way society has developed over the years, because of culture, because of history. That's how it's been but it's changing fairly fast. I am just behind the curve.

G: But are you saying that society basically dictates that women should do caring roles?

A: Historically, yes, when I was at school we weren't taught domestic science, we didn't get that. Girls did. 'A woman's work is never done.' That's a saying... Men make the money, do the hunting, lead businesses, and the women have children and they raise them. I'm not saying that is right, because it's not, and it will change, but you have to fight for that change to happen.

G: So when you and Mum decided to have kids, did you have any conscious decision-making to be, like, 'I don't want my kids to grow up with these gender ideas'?

A: Not really, no. But I think we did treat you differently to them. They think we spoiled you, but we definitely also made you do more around the house.

My dad pauses, to reflect on what he has done to make our household cleaner.

A: I was good at some stuff, I did change the nappies, I did get up in the night. But, look, I am not remotely proud of my general lack of housework abilities.

G: Do you think we are reverting back to a more misogynistic time?

A: Yes. And by the way I have always hated misogyny. Part of this whole populist, nationalist right-wing agenda is tied in with misogyny. You see it with Russia, see it with Trump. It's almost like they're saying women are getting above their station, and similar with black people; these right-wing populists don't like it when [people] who aren't like them get power. You know, why did Putin soften all of that stuff about domestic violence? Well, he's a strong male leader who wants men to like him – and part of men feeling strong is feeling they have ownership of their wives and that they can hit them.

G: Trump and Boris Johnson also have questionable views on race and gender.

A: Most right-minded mainstream, liberal people, when the video came out of Trump [talking about] grabbing the woman 'by the pussy' – they thought he was done then, or 'that's going to really damage him'. I actually think it helped him. Bigly.

G: Agreed. When you say most of us, I think that's because we're in a bubble, and far removed from the people who actually respected this about Trump.

G: Do you think, fifty years from now, granted the world hasn't ended, that men will hold fewer positions of power?

A: I have just read a French book [*Le monde des nouveaux auto-ritaires* by Michel Duclos] about the slide to populist nationalist and authoritarian leaders around the world. Lots of them. All of them men. I think we have made a lot of progress but I think at the moment we are going backwards. And don't forget Merkel is about to go. Also there has been progress in business and media but WE ARE still way off genuine parity between men and women. So I think there will only be progress if there is a genuine backlash among men and women to the kind of global leadership people seem to be going for.

G: If you could change one thing about men in the future what would it be?

A: If there was one thing I would change it is that they just give up on the general belief, which I think many men still hold, that they are superior.

This conversation with my dad is a conversation that we've been having ongoing throughout the years. It has always stifled me that he knows where he's lacking around the house and still doesn't pick up slack where it might help. However, right after we stopped officially doing the interview, I had a realisation.

My dad went on a rant about clutter in the house, and he started to clean up what he calls my mum's and my mess. He wasn't doing this in a 'look at me' way, he was doing this because he genuinely hates clutter. And I realised that that is something.

I CAN BE SEXIST, TOO

I have a confession to make. This is something I am really not proud of, and something that it's taken me years to come to terms with.

When I was eighteen years old I fell in love for the first time. I was on my gap year (I'm sorry, I hate me, too). I had decided to go travelling on my own because I knew that going away for months with any of my friends, even though I love them (BFFE and all that), would just result in murder, and I was too young to die, or spend my life in jail.

I was travelling in the Caribbean, because I also didn't want to risk bumping into any of my basic friends in Thailand, Cambodia or Brazil. The first place I went to was Guadeloupe. The second place I went to was Puerto Rico. On my first day there, I met a man.

On my second day there, the man and I had moved in together. Fast. Freaky. Thinking about it now, that was very creepy. I was eighteen, and the man was thirty-two. Fourteen years for anyone who can't do maths.

We were together for a really intense month and then we parted ways. When I left him I was sad. But also I was a wide-eyed eighteen-year-old, so not long after I left him for Jamaica I realised he wasn't the love of my life, he just had a really nice house in the centre of San Juan, and it was all quite exciting. I liked that I was living a movie romance IRL.

Unfortunately, by the time I had this realisation, I had already agreed that I would go back and see the man in Puerto Rico before I travelled back to London.

I knew I didn't want to go back. I was having fun in other places... if you know what I mean.

But I felt I owed it to him to go back and say goodbye.

I'm sure Greta Thunberg wouldn't approve of the carbon emissions of this love story but, reader, I went back to Puerto Rico. Five minutes after I arrived I decided I had to leave. I texted my best friend Anna, who was at a house party in Leeds, and she booked me a BA flight out of Puerto Rico back to Miami. I did go and see him but it was only to tell him that I wouldn't be staying long as I had a flight to catch, and I was super-sorry, I thought I loved him but, unusually for me, I was wrong.

I was in Puerto Rico for precisely four hours and twenty-seven minutes. Up until this part of the story I am proud of how I handled things. I'm proud I had the courage to get out of something that I wasn't vibesing. I'm proud I went back to tell him face to face rather than ghost him or send him a wimpish little text.

But the part of the story I'm not proud of is how I felt when I told him that I was leaving, and he burst into tears.

This wasn't just a little bit of tears but like crying at the end of *The Notebook* level. If you don't know what that means... I don't know what to say.

He cried and cried and cried and cried. And I thought it was pathetic. At the time, I'd never seen a man cry. My dad always tended to hide away when he was depressed, and I did see him cry at his mum's funeral after this.

But aged eighteen I'd thought that men crying genuinely was a bad thing. I had internalised Pat so deeply that when I was watching a man cry because I was dumping him and hurting his feelings, instead of comforting him because I had caused him this pain, I told him to stop crying. What a fucking bitch I was.

I realised years later that this was me being sexist, and I decided that the next time a man cried in front of me I would celebrate it. So a year later I dumped a guy (this sounds like I've dumped a lot of people; I really haven't, I've been dumped LOADS), and he DIDN'T EVEN CRY. His eyes were so dry I could see sand dunes forming in them.

I'd hyped myself up for him to cry because I was, like, he's gonna cry, and I'm gonna support him and make him feel really good, and I, single-handedly, am gonna change the whole narrative of men crying. But he didn't cry. I asked him why he wasn't crying and he said, 'Grace, I don't like you *that* much.'

THE DOUBLE STANDARDS OF WESTMINSTER

On 29 February 2020, Boris Johnson revealed that he and his fiancée, Carrie Symonds, were expecting their first child together and would be getting married. Ah, how lovely for them, said most of the British newspapers who have backed Brexit and Johnson's journey to prime minister. A baby is harmless news and, of course, we should be happy for Symonds and her future child. Even though it is really SO hard to imagine her ever wanting to have actual intercourse with Boris Johnson. Who knows what STDs he may have.

But it is hard to look at Johnson's pregnancy announcement without the broader context of Boris Johnson's shagging history.

Boris Johnson has been a slag for many years. If that word offends you, I'm sorry. I've been called a slag in my life and I know it offends some, but what offends me more is this:

Imagine if our prime minister had been a woman. A woman who had left her husband for a much younger man. A woman who, while her ex was having cancer treatment, announced a pregnancy and wedding weeks after her last divorce had been finalised. The word slag would be trending on Twitter. It would be on the cover of the *Sun*. Her ability to lead would be taken away.

The word slag doesn't need to be an insult. But the double standards to which we hold men and women insult us all.

The country would not be so forgiving if Margaret Thatcher's or Theresa May's private lives had been even an ounce as fruitful. But Boris Johnson, amidst all this and more, won an election. He won an election after refusing to state how many children he has. He clearly has no idea how many children he has.

But can you imagine if a woman leader refused to state how many children she has? She'd have a Channel 5 documentary about her called *How Many Children Does this Woman Have?* She would certainly not be living in Downing Street with hubby #3.

Our interest in politicians' personal lives isn't necessarily healthy, but it makes me angry that the public and media let someone like Boris Johnson get away with all of the above when I am sure they would hound a woman or a person of colour for doing the same. But we're conditioned to place women under impossible scrutiny, while men simply have to do the bare minimum.

We all thought that when the Donald Trump 'grab her by the pussy' tape came out, it was game over for him as a presidential contender. But it wasn't.

Again, let's reverse this. Imagine if a tape had emerged of Hillary Clinton bragging about being famous, and how that allows her to 'grab men by the dick'. This would have been used to completely ruin her character and ability to lead the country.

Many factors determined the outcome of the 2016 presidential race. But let's face it: Trump stood accused by many women of sexual assault, and had repeatedly demonstrated ingrained racism and misogyny. Meanwhile, Hillary had a private email account and she may as well have done worse than Trump and then some. Trump won.

Let me be clear about this: I think that there are many brilliant, inspiring, talented people in politics and activism who make me truly hopeful for the future. But unfortunately, time and time again, it's the Johnsons and the Trumps who stay at the top of the chain. These men personify the worst aspects of maleness – lack of empathy; a belief that they have a right to lie; colossal privilege; irresponsibility; narcissism – and yet the public elects them, entrusts them with all of our futures, and sees hiccups as just part of their personas.

And there is a real danger of being implicit in the political success of men like this. We're growing habituated to men who get away with things like sexual assault, racism and misogyny. Habituation can breed despairing resignation. But our response should be precisely the opposite. We should demand more of men, not less. This can be difficult when we're in a society which seems to support these kinds of men, but our roles should be to scrutinise them as much as our power lets us, and, more importantly, influence other men, young men in particular, to see these Trumpian and Johnson-esque behaviours and attitudes as weak, in the hope that we will then influence the next generation to break this vicious cycle of toxic men.

LET'S HEAR IT FROM THE BOYS

Maybe a lot of men think that the bar has risen too high for them. They have to be good dads and sons, while also being breadwinners. They are expected to be physically fit and good-looking – while not seeming to care too much about their personal grooming. They can't go bald (apparently that's a real no-no nowadays)! They have to not be perverts (that's really hard, apparently). And they must be fluent in the unwritten languages and codes of consent before they try it on with us.

In 2018 I met my boyfriend Idrisa. Idrisa is five years older than me. This is something my honorary sisters Georgia and Grace Gould told me I needed to find, because they reckoned men the same age as me were incapable of handling me.

Idrisa was born in Nigeria, and moved to London with his family when he was nine. He went to boarding school in the

UK, and he studied science and other clever-sounding stuff at university and for his masters.

We are different in many ways. Different race, gender, education style. He is private, and modest. I am loud and boastful of my brilliance. He doesn't have social media. I confess every element of my life to my Instagram followers. If it hadn't been for a dating app called Hinge, I doubt our paths would ever have crossed.

Hinge, if you're reading this, please sponsor me? Mine and my boyfriend's love story has been brilliant promotion for your app.

When I met Idrisa, I knew instantly that he was different from a lot of men. I could tell he was sort of a lad but with a sensitive understanding of women. He's hilarious, and always makes me laugh loads, but he's also not bothered about the fact that I am the funnier one.

Our relationship has not always been easy. My mum and dad both think he deserves a medal for always very calmly and pragmatically handling my tumultuous anxiety and hypochondria.

We've both taught each other a huge amount. He's shown me a different version of being a man that I hadn't really known before, and so I wanted to chat to him for this. It's a bit weird interviewing your boyfriend, but relationships are weird, so here we go.

IDRISA

Grace: Would you say you're a lad?

Idrisa: I think I can be a lad at times. But I don't think all elements of being a lad are bad.

G: Like what?

I: Like being into sport, some elements of the humour. I don't think they're bad things. The more toxic stereotypes of lads, I loathe.

G: My dad defined toxic masculinity as when men become brutish and offensive. How would you define it?

I: When men consistently make bad decisions because they don't want to let down other men, or appear weak in front of other men.

G: So it's peer pressure?

I: Partly, yes.

G: Why are men more prone to violence?

I: As a man growing up, what do you see other men do? It's a cycle that continues. If a fifteen-year-old goes to a pub now in a rowdy area, on a weekend, he'll see dudes acting like that and then they might want to act like that – because they think that's what you're supposed to do. Plus, when you're pissed, your inhibitions are lower.

G: Do you think men have pressures – like, if they don't like football, men see them as less of a man?

I: I think it's less pressure, and more a way to connect with other men. When you meet someone, you really want to talk about something. Every guy I've made friends with since school, we've all bonded over football.

G: That's how you bonded with my dad. When we went to Arsenal v. Burnley.

I: Yeah, I mean we were supporting the opposing teams but it was a good day.

G: Would you say the way you and your friends have spoken about women since school has changed?

I: I'd say the way we judge people generally has changed... When I was at school, I just cared about sports, and having girls as friends, but didn't really care about having a girlfriend, or sex. My friends weren't typical high-testosterone guys. But, yeah, the way we talk about women has changed. I always cared more about personalities, but my friends would have cared way more about looks. That's changed, thankfully.

G: Do you think men feel confused around the boundaries of flirting with women since #metoo?

I: I think men will take fewer risks because they're worried about what will be said. But by and large the majority of men who know how to flirt properly don't need to change.

G: What is proper flirting?

I: Knowing that you're never making the other person uncomfortable. Like there has been a shift in behaviour from men who knew that the stuff they were doing was questionable. The defensive people are the ones who have done bad stuff and feel persecuted for it now, and they feel people are retrospectively judging them for it. They're the ones who will really have to change.

G: Have you observed fathers and mums being treated differently in terms of the expectations?

I: Absolutely. I do get how difficult parenting is. But I've seen people basically want to give dads who push their kids in a buggy an OBE, and women who do the same get no reward. Women can close a pushchair with one hand while breastfeeding... and talking. That's incredible, and they deserve more credit. Growing up, there were a few of my friends whose dads had left them. But we only had one friend who lived with just their dad, because their mum had left. And we were all like, 'WTF, how could she, a mum, leave?' Whereas men do that all the time and you don't question it.

G: Do you think women's and men's sexual histories are treated differently?

I: 100 per cent.

G: Why does it happen?

I: I think some men grow up thinking that a woman's sexuality is precious and a man's isn't. So a woman should keep hers guarded, and a man should do whatever the hell he wants. Also in films and books and stories the idea that a woman having sex with someone means more than when a man does is perpetuated.

G: What were your first impressions of feminism?

I: I thought a feminist was strictly a woman, a white woman – because they were the only ones talking about it, that I saw.

G: Do you see it's not that now?

I: Now I get what feminists are actually fighting for, then I see that it can be anyone. But if you don't understand what they're trying to do, then you're going to have a stereotype of what they are.

G: Do you think a man can be a feminist?

I: Define 'feminism'.

G: Men and women should be equal.

I: If that's your definition, then, yes, a man can be one.

G: Are you one?

I: I don't want to say I'm one.

G: Why?

I: Because I don't like when men say they're feminists for show.

G: But you're not doing it for show, you are very feminist in the way you live your life.

I: Am I. How?

G: You believe in equality, and not for show; you truly believe it, that I should be as successful as a man; you believe men and women should share parenting. You do everything around the house. You cook. You don't speak about women in a derogatory way. You stand up for women. That, to me, is a feminist.

I: OK. I am a feminist.

G: Why don't you cry much? Do you see it as a weakness?

I: I do cry occasionally. Kobe Bryant's death [has] made me very upset. I don't see it as a weakness, I just don't like doing it personally. If I saw a man crying I wouldn't be, like, you're weak. I just don't think crying has the healing powers for me that it does for other people.

G: What do you think you'll be like as a dad?

I: I think I'll be 50:50.

G: What about 60:40?

I: If needs be. If I need to pick up the slack of a lazy [whispers] feminist then, yeah, I can do that. No, I understand the importance of men doing housework. Women push the baby out of them – the least we can do is make sure the house is nice and they're fed.

G: How did your mum raise you to be a man? Did she teach you to act like a man?

I: No, she didn't. She grew up in a family where she'd seen that [acting like a man] as a burden. When men were told to 'be a man', it ended up disastrously, so that wasn't how she encouraged us to be.

G: You were born in Nigeria and moved here when you were nine. How is it different here to Nigeria in terms of male roles?

I: Men's roles in Nigeria are set in stone. It would be a crime for a man to be a stay-at-home dad.

G: Would your mum say she's a feminist?

I: My mum and her friends... I don't think they'd call themselves feminists because, to them, that word is associated with white women. Nigerian women might see it more as, like: just get on with it and prove it with your actions. Prove you can do it, and not necessarily fight the system.

G: What men give you hope for the future?

I: A lot of athletes. Reggie Bullock. His sister was trans and she got murdered, he's done a lot of work around that. Dwyane Wade, kid is trans and he's been really amazing on that. In terms of being a man, athletes do represent a lot of masculinity, and when they're making positive decisions it gives men good role models. I don't have much hope with politicians, they're just less believable and authentic. They're pretending to be real people but I don't buy it.

G: If you could change one thing about men in the future, what would it be?

I: I would like them to stop assaulting people, women. I would like them to stop this harassment and online abuse, because that is time and time again being done by men.

A lot of this conversation with Idrisa felt really familiar, and like things we've discussed a lot. But other parts weren't. I like that he admits to not wanting to call himself a feminist because of the bad stereotypes of men using feminism to get girls, and also because of the impression he's always had of feminism being a thing for white women. This is important to know, and for us white women to work to change.

I also think this is an important example of how men can be feminists without wearing it on their t-shirts. Idrisa had a different idea of feminism growing up, and I totally get why he doesn't feel it's particularly him, but I also think his mum has raised him to be a brilliant man who, whether he says it or not, really is a feminist.

SCHOOL

The first time I remember feeling distinctly different from boys was when I started secondary school. I had grown up with two brothers, Rory and Calum, who are seven and six years older than me. Growing up, I wasn't hyper-aware of the gender differences between us. But then suddenly I was fourteen and I had a pair of double J breasts and my perception of gender totally changed forever.

I went to a comprehensive girls' school in Camden, north London, called Parliament Hill School. Fun fact: Dua Lipa went to Parliament Hill School with me. Funner fact: I thought I would be more famous than her. She won.

Next door to my secondary school was a boys' school that my brothers attended. William Ellis School. Sounds so manly, doesn't it? Willies! At Willie Ellis, they wore uniforms. At Parliament Hill, we didn't. We expressed ourselves through short skirts and very big quiffs. Our appearance seemed to matter more. I went from never being valued according to how I looked to suddenly being valued in precisely that way, sometimes by boys I'd known my whole life from living in the same area and going to the same primary schools.

Meanwhile, in certain ways, we were learning very different things. Periods for us. Wanking for them. Girls were teaching other girls what they'd heard from older girls, or in magazines: pubes are a no-no. Wanking is weird. Only boys can do that and sex has to be done with boys. Boys like it if you are a bit more stupid than them. They like it even more if you flatter them about things like their shoelaces. There was a general idea that we were working towards when we'd be able to go out for lunch in year nine and actually get real-life attention from boys. Attention from boys was like oxygen to us.

I feel lucky to have gone to a girls' school. Statistically girls do better when they're educated with girls, while boys do better when they're educated with girls.

This suggests that there are performative pressures at work in co-education. Subconsciously or otherwise, girls don't want to seem as clever as boys, because they don't want to threaten their self-esteem. They make themselves smaller – which in turn makes the boys bigger.

I recently met a group of thirteen-year-old girls. That sounds creepy. They're my friend's child and her friends. I asked these thirteen-year-old girls what the boys at their school are like. 'Annoying,' they replied. 'They do this thing, when they want to tell us to shut up, where they tell us to get back in the kitchen – or make them a sandwich.' This may or may not shock you. It shocked me, not because I was surprised that the words 'get back in the kitchen' are still being spoken, but more that they're being spoken by boys at such a young age.

The words 'sandwich' and 'kitchen' are words that a lot of feminists have to block on their Instagram feeds, because Internet trolls think that this is a fantastically witty riposte to what we have to say.

But in schools? How is this vernacular reaching pre-pubescent teens? I went onto the Internet to try and work it out. 'Get back in the kitchen' is a phrase that comes up a lot on Internet forums that are dominated by incel-type men. Then I read further, and a lot of the incels that I've referred to earlier play on video games. Who else plays on video games? Teenage boys! And they chat to these older people who introduce them to this old-school language. I'm sure some of them also hear this language at home. But what saddens me is that most of the boys who tell their female peers to get back into the kitchen don't actually know what they're implying. That doesn't mean it's okay, but it also doesn't make them awful people.

So, gender inequality is still being bred in schools, in the same way that it was when I was there ten years ago. Sadly, a lot of girls need the luxury I had, of being in an all-girls' school.

This is a dilemma for me. I do think the school system breaks up genders too extremely, and that we should hope to get to a place in the future where genders are much less entrenched in the schooling system. But I also feel that I personally benefited from being at a girls' school. Parliament Hill School was incredibly diverse; it was like a feminist utopia where we all felt that we could achieve everything despite our gender, class or race. I wonder if being educated with boys would have dragged this spirit down because we may have been caught up in playing the stereotypes? Would Dua Lipa be as successful if she had been in a co-ed school? Would she have written as many powerful feminist ballads had she not had that girl spirit in her?

However, I feel that co-education is really important for LGBTQI+ kids, who may feel totally lost in a same-sex school. One of my best friends, Jack, also from my local area, was at Acland Burghley School, a co-ed state school in north-west London. I know that Jack's experience at this school was much better because he was educated around women.

Now that you've heard from my dad and my boyfriend, I want you to hear from Jack. Firstly, because he's one of my favourite people in the world, but, secondly, because as a gay man Jack has a really different perspective on being a man.

Jack and I have been friends since secondary school. We became friends when we were around fourteen. We were part of a larger group of friends (boys and girls) who went to three schools in our local area. Jack was a sort of bridge between the girls and the boys. He came out when we were seventeen. He was actually outed by someone else, which is not what he wanted. Just a note to anyone who thinks it is their right to out people: it's not, it's their decision and you doing it for them means that they and all of their friends will think you're an awful person, forever.

JACK

Grace: Having you as a best friend since I was fourteen has been a really interesting insight into men. You're a gay man, but you didn't come out till we were seventeen. However, I've always felt that all of the straight guys would use you as a gateway to explore and find out about LGBTQI+ people. Have you noticed this before? And does it annoy you?

Jack: Always. When we were growing up, any LGBTQI+ query, the boys would ask me. They'd see other people, a trans friend of mine, or drag queens. And they'd ask me all of these questions about it. I got bored of it. And it's stopped – I think we all grew up, and we got out of the bubble and everyone met more LGBTQI+ people. So then I wasn't the only one.

G: I think you'd agree with me when I say you were always the bridge between the straight boys and us girls, who were at the time all straight?

J: Yeah, it was weird. Because of my mum's work as a manager of various Soho restaurants in the eighties, she had loads of gay friends, so I had loads of gay older people in my life, but no one my age. I think it came from our group of friends being a 50:50 mix. One of the reasons why I think our male friends are pretty good guys is because we – me and you girls – helped them [boys] understand how to be sensitive with women. When boys are friends with girls they understand their feelings, their experiences; they're more compassionate.

G: Agreed. That's definitely one of the perks of Idrisa: he's had a lot of close female friends and is so sensitive to women. How would you define 'toxic masculinity'?

J: It's ego-driven, my dick's bigger than yours. When you see two men in a fight at the pub, one puffs out their chest. I have traits of toxic masculinity. I think it stems down to an ego, a fear of weakness. It doesn't have to be a physical situation, it could be a work situation where you're not willing to be okay with something if you think you're right.

G: What was it like for you coming out? When did you?

J: Seventeen. It was easy actually, on reflection. That girl outed me before I had come out.

G: We won't speak her name.

J: No, but she told everyone, and obviously everyone knew. No one gave a shit. Unexpected people would say: 'Oh, it's so cool that you're happy to be comfortable around us' – which, looking back on it, isn't that cool.

G: How was your experience at school?

J: Got bullied. Not for being gay, but for being different. There were never gay slurs.

G: How did your dad react?

J: Not great, and I was confused – he and my mum have lots of gay friends. Now we talk about it loads, and it's totally fine. Eventually I got it out of him that he was weird because he was scared that I was going to be in a domestic abusive relationship with another man. He was worried it was going to make my life harder.

G: And what about your stepdad?

J: My stepdad and my mum had a bet when I was five that I was gay. He said I was, she said I wasn't. Barney, my stepdad, is posh and that poshness allows for some more camp behaviour sometimes – whereas my dad is a south London geezer.

G: Queer fashion is sort of being appropriated by straight men at the moment. What does this make you feel and why do you think this is happening?

J: Because gay men always dress better than straight men. Fashion in itself is becoming genderless. For the past ten years, dressing more casual has come in a bit – that takes you away from the suit, which we still see as very masculine.

G: Were there people there who found your comfortability with your sexuality threatening?

J: I can definitely tell when there's an energy. Because I don't have to prove anything to anyone, I'm just me, and that intimidates a lot of people who aren't comfortable with themselves. I had to come to terms with that ten years ago. When you come out as gay you're going to lose respect from some people and they're going to think of you differently. You just lose those people from your life, and you learn to be yourself, whereas straight men still feel they're performing their masculinity. It's a masculine front. It's a costume. And you can always tell when people aren't comfortable with it.

G: Who were your role models growing up?

J: I was obsessed with fashion, went and worked in it, used to love Grace Coddington. I know now why I loved her, because she was making stories and it was all her idea; she created the whole vision. That's always been a thing for me, in anything I do. I want to birth the idea and finish it myself. And Vivienne Westwood – she was so punk and didn't give a shit. I used to wear kilts to school.

G: Do you think there's room for improvement when it comes to men?

J: I think the whole thing about it for me is this need for

them to learn compassion – and I do think that women are much more emotionally in tune. At no point in Personal, Social and Health Education did we get taught to be compassionate. I think it would be really useful for boys to learn compassion, and sensitivity. There's no weakness in being sensitive. You can still be a man and cry.

G: How can we improve the process of boys turning into men at school?

J: I think maybe a healthy, rounded introduction to various types of people is always helpful. And I don't even mean like lessons about people's cultures. I think more and really diverse stuff from all walks of life and a place where they are celebrated for that would help young boys and girls really move into the world more compassionate and understanding towards everyone.

G: How do you feel it could have been better in terms of LGBTQI+ education? When it comes to that part of education, I just didn't have any. We need an education on LGBTQI+ and everything around it, simple and easy. We need to talk about all sex and take away any stigmas. Teachers need to explain things and be able to answer some of the tricky questions.

G: Are you a feminist?

J: Yes.

G: Do you feel welcomed into feminism?

J: Yes, I do. I think if you've got the right intentions – things like the Pink Protest – as long as you're there for the right reasons, of course they're going to welcome you.

G: If you could change one thing about men in the future what would it be?

J: Make them all hot and in love with me.

MARKETING FEMINISM TO MEN; A BIT LIKE A PROTEIN SHAKE

I want to tell you about a thing called War Paint. It sounds very manly, right? Like something that men might buy to make their dick bigger? War Paint is a make-up brand for men. On all of War Paint's branding, they want you to know that this is make-up 'FOR MEN'. Their Instagram handle is @warpaintformen. War Paint is trying very hard to distance itself from feminine make-up brands.

In reality, their products are exactly the same as those used by women: concealer, foundation, bronzer, brushes. But it's presented in the same way that men's razors are packaged in contrast to women's – minimalistic, masculine and discreet.

War Paint for men is a make-up brand that has marketed itself perfectly for men. And I don't think this is a bad thing. Men should be allowed to wear make-up, too (men don't have perfect skin, you know). But most heterosexual men don't feel comfortable walking into Benefit and buying a 'Cheekleaders' blush set, or the 'Hello Flawless' foundation. They're nervous about wearing make-up to begin with, because they've probably been told that men wearing make-up is 'gay', or makes them look weak.

The very existence of War Paint for men suggests that there is a demand for male make-up. It's branding also suggests that buying make-up from more feminine brands is a step too far. All of which got me thinking about how men need things to be packaged in a certain way for them to consume. As I said before, they are simple creatures, but I do love them! #notallmen, but some.

I asked my three interviewees if they would ever wear make-up:

Dad: Only on telly and only if they say I need it for the lights.

Idrisa: No.

Jack: Erm, yes, why should you get to cover up your spots and I can't?

Heed this: packaging matters to men. We are seeing, for instance, an increasing number of employers who offer flexible working schemes – but too often they are targeted at women, and associated with being on the 'mummy track'. We need to tackle this 'flexibility stigma', and the most straightforward way to do so would be to encourage more men directly to take on part-time and flexible work and discourage the notion that doing so is somehow a betrayal of their masculinity.

Remember: they will only buy into it if it makes the testosterone in their body bubble.

SON

The year is 2040. I have a fifteen-year-old son and a seventeen-year-old daughter. We live in a really nice house which is powered by solar panels (that's the law now, thanks to our new environmentalist prime minister who came to power after the brief apocalypse).

I'm making my son do an interview with me, to try and find out what being a young man is like now, twenty years on from when I've written this. His name will remain a mystery.

Grace: So... what's it like having me as a mum?

Son: Fine. But I wish you'd stop speaking about me in your comedy. It's creepy.

Grace: I can't resist! You're so funny! Do you feel like you and your sister are very different?

Son: Not really. I mean. She's definitely tougher than me.

Grace: What do you mean?

Son: She's braver. She's not scared of anything.

Grace: What are you scared of?

Son: I'm scared the world's gonna end because of climate change. And that we could have prevented it. I'm scared that you or Dad are gonna die. Scared of doing bad at school.

Grace: You're a lot like me when I was your age.

Son: What changed?

Grace: When you get older you have more perspective, and I am now less anxious about things that are out of my control. How do you channel those fears?

Son: Well, I dunno. I talk. To you guys, and friends.

Grace: What do you and your friends like to do when you're hanging out?

Son: Just stuff.

Grace: Do you talk about your fears with them?

Son: Yeah, with some of them. Some of them will laugh if you try to talk 'bout emotions, but there are a couple I will talk to.

Grace: Why do you think they laugh?

Son: Dunno, maybe because if they don't they'd cry.

Grace: Do you feel you know enough about sex?

Son: For God's sake, Mum. Of course I do. I've been living with you.

VICTORY!!

Grace: Do you feel you could ask questions about it?

Son: I guess.

Grace: When I was younger, which wasn't very long ago, women were still very much unfairly treated.

Son: How?

Grace: They were paid less. They weren't protected by laws when it came to domestic abuse and sexual violence. All over the world they were treated like property.

Son: Has that gone away now?

Grace: A bit. It's not gone away, but it's definitely improved. When I was in my twenties the world seemed to be going back in time, and it was only countries like Denmark and Norway that were properly progressing gender equality. Then we had this awful prime minister called Boris Johnson who was not only awful in his opinions and personal life, but was actually TERRIBLE at leading during the coronavirus and the financial crash. After that it was like young people and millennials were so outraged, and they were a huge part of the population, and that started to shift the electorate. And slowly parliament has become nearly 50:50.

Son: I think it's still not equal enough. I still think girls are unfairly treated at school.

Grace: How?

Son: Boys try and call them stupid.

Grace: And do the girls know they're just doing that because they're insecure?

Son: Yeah, the girls are great at ignoring it, and I think boys who do that are seen as quite embarrassing.

Grace: How do you imagine your life in twenty years?

Son: Mum, the world is sinking! There won't be a life then.

Grace: I know, I know. But listen, there is some hope. More is being done to prevent that than when I was your age.

Son: Yeah, but it's too late!

Grace: But when I was your age, genuinely most leaders denied climate change was even real. Can you imagine that?!

Son: That makes me feel sad.

Grace: Well, exactly. But they were forced to learn. And when my generation got older, things started to change, because we thought in a much different way than our parents. I like the way that you and your friends explore your gender expression. Does that feel normal to you?

Son: We don't really care about picking labels.

Grace: That's very liberating. That was definitely harder when I was at school.

Son: Sorry to hear that.

Grace: Are you a feminist?

Son: Yes, Mum. Can I ask you a question?

Grace: Always.

Son: Were you ever as scared as I am about the future?

Grace: I was scared so much of the time. I grew up in a family which was for a lot of time in the limelight, and there were people who really didn't like your grandpa. That made me incredibly anxious. So did sexism, and the fears that I had of men attacking me, which I worry your sister still has. I was scared for minorities in this country, still am. There is so much to be scared of, all the time. But there is so much to be hopeful for. When I was about twenty-one I realised that when you feel despair, you have to channel that into making some form of positive change. You and your peers give me hope for that – you're always starting campaigns at

school. And you have to hold onto that hope, and
that passion you have, promise me?

Son: Promise.

I hope my son is as lovely as him, because I am so excited to
meet him. He seems much more in tune with the feminine
than boys I knew at fifteen. He doesn't seem to mind that his
older sister is the braver one of the two. He is surrounded by
other young people who seem to be breaking down the gender barriers, which is great. My son wears nail polish, and
loves football. He combines the masculine with the feminine.
He challenges me and his father everyday to rethink things
that even I haven't thought about.

He gives me hope for the future of men because he is the
product of the world he is growing up in, a world in which his
dad is more active around the house than his mum. A world
where women, people of colour and the LGBTQI+ community have the space to represent themselves and are listened
to when they speak.

He has also grown up in a world that is truly afraid. He
and his peers care so much about the environment, and they
are angry that not enough has been done. They are the generation that Greta Thunberg inspired, and they are infiltrat-
ing all parts of society.

The far right is still alive and kicking, but the Internet has now got real legislation that social media sites are supposed to stick to. Granted they don't always abide by those rules, but we're getting there, and political fake news ads on Facebook are a part of history, thank goodness.

This is what I hope the future of men is: one where men can be vulnerable, and weak. A world where men aren't afraid of letting some of the power go and giving it to other people, because in the long term that will make the world a better place.

MEN AREN'T TRASH – THEY'RE RECYCLING

It now comes to the point in this essay where I have somehow to find a way to close. I have spent a lot of time, ten hours a week, I'd say, writing this. And I've thought a lot about what it is that I'm trying to say, and it's this:

Men aren't trash, they're recycling.

'Men are trash' is a phrase used commonly today to describe the waste of space that a lot of men take up. It's the antidote to Not All Men of the Internet age. It's a way for people, women mainly, to express their anger about men's behaviour. For example, when men get caught cheating, they'll be described as trash. When men take advantage of women, they are trash.

Donald Trump = Donald Trash.

I've observed a lot of trashy men in the world since I was pretty young. I remember, on my first day of primary school, a boy called me fat, and then, when I retaliated by pouring water on him, he went to the headteacher and told the headteacher that I had hit him. I got in loads of trouble, and he got in none. That was trash behaviour.

But how useful is the notion that men are trash? While I understand the health benefits of expressing a collective contempt for men, I think long term, when we continue to exist with men, when we continue to be in relationships with them, perhaps we could find another way to move things forward a bit.

This is why I think we should start saying that men aren't trash, they're recycling. It is not a woman's responsibility to teach and raise boys into men; however, we could get a lot more done if we break down the divide between all genders. I don't think men are trash; I don't think they're a complete waste to the world. If we think of recycling as the process of converting waste into reusable material, that's exactly what we need to do to men. We need to convert their waste-of-space parts into reusable aspects.

If this essay could do one thing, it would be to encourage men to be feminists. To encourage men to be allies to ALL women. Not just the women you know. All women. And it would be to show men that they can really benefit from feminism too.

And so here is my *pièce de résistance*. My manifesto:

TEN WAYS FEMINISM IS FUN FOR MEN

1) SEX – Feminism is great for your sex life. I am sure my boyfriend could vouch for this. Firstly, you don't have to be afraid of asking for a finger up the bum; a feminist won't judge you for that. But, also, feminists are more likely to have educated themselves on sex via proper feminist porn, which demonstrates what sex actually looks like. This means they'll know how to make themselves and YOU cum! Feminism wants equality of opportunity, and equality of orgasms! Because sex really isn't fun when only one of you is getting to the climax.

2) MONEY – I'm not saying men only care about money because, actually, I am far more money-obsessed than any man in my life. My greatest goal in life is to be so rich that I never have to fly Ryanair again. But listen, lads, feminism can save you money. When you're dating a feminist, you don't have to pay for everything on a date! In fact, your date will get pissed off if you even try to pay for everything. So,

equality AND more money in ya pocket! Plus, feminism wants men to not have to bear the burden of being the presumptive breadwinner, which means that a lot of the fears men have around money will be saved.

3) FREEDOM – The women in your life will have more freedom and choices because of feminism. Your daughters, future daughters, nieces, granddaughters – don't you want them to have the same freedoms as all men do? As I said at the beginning of this essay, there are millions of women all over the world being held back because of their gender; you could play a part in changing that.

4) FASHION – Feminism will help men express themselves in any way they want to. Men can wear all the make-up in the world, or not, and still identify as a heterosexual man, if that's what they want to do. Feminism will allow men to embrace the nuances of being a human.

5) FLEXIBILITY – Not just in sex. Wink wink wank wank. Feminism wants to make working hours more flexible for everyone. Globally, almost three-quarters of all people (72 per cent – REAL SURVEY) agree that employers should make it easier for men to combine childcare with work. Whether or not men know it now, their lives and their

relationships with their families would be better off once flexible working is truly embraced. Surely fathers want flexible working hours just as much as mothers? There is also plenty of research showing that flexible working increases productivity, as better work/life balance leads to happier, more effective workers, ergo MORE MONEY!

6) HAPPINESS – Feminism wants men to live their best lives. Free to talk about their emotions and express themselves without judgement from society. Suicide is the biggest killer for men under the age of forty-five. Why is this? Because men internalise their worries, mental health and pressures until they can't cope with anything anymore. They are less likely than women to seek medical help for depression (indeed, medical help for anything). Instead, they tend to self-medicate – with sometimes catastrophic consequences.

7) MEANINGFUL RELATIONSHIPS – Men could worry less about being a 'real man' and put more time into creating meaningful relationships with the people around them! How nice would bonding be when you aren't preoccupied with putting on a masculine front?

8) CONSENT – Feminism would help men not be rapists! I know it already has! Feminism teaches men that they have

absolutely zero power over women's bodies and therefore have no right to abuse women in any way. Absolutely nobody likes a rapist so...

9) NO SHAME – A huge part of intersectional feminism is that we don't just care about the women we know, but all women, and LGBTQI+ folk. We want to live in a world where all people are free from shame around their sexuality, men included. Historically, men have been discriminated against if they aren't heterosexual. Gay men have been through so much toxic abuse and oppression over centuries, and for me a huge part of men and feminism is moving society towards a place where men don't have to feel ashamed of who they are.

10) LEADERS – Most leaders around the world right now are men. What's more, all authoritarian leaders are men. If we look at the state of the world, it's clear that just giving men the power is not working. A key part of equality is that we allow leaders and bosses to represent the people that they are leading. Whether this is in politics, business, sport or technology, feminism wants to dismantle the tradition of the same old posh rich straight middle-aged I just nodded off there I got SO bored, SAME OLD MEN in leading positions. If we got equality, we could diversify leadership roles and

leaders would be more dynamic, and in the long run improve the state of the nation. Ultimately, in this country, we need the days of Etonian men leading EVERYTHING to be over so that we can finally have some equal and new-fashioned FUN.

AFTERWORD

In 1924, inspired by a sensational essay they had published the previous year, the publishers Kegan Paul launched a series of small, elegant books called To-Day and To-Morrow. The founding essay was *Daedalus; or, Science and the Future*, and its author, the biologist J. B. S. Haldane, made several striking predictions: genetic modification, wind power, artificial food. But the idea that captured the imagination of his contemporaries was what he called 'ectogenesis' – the gestation of embryos in artificial wombs. Haldane's friend Aldous Huxley included it in his novel *Brave New World*, in which humans are cloned and mass-produced in 'Hatcheries' (it was Haldane who later gave us the word 'clone'). Fast-forward almost a century, and scientists have now trialled ectogenesis on sheep and are exploring its potential for saving dangerously premature babies.

Haldane took no prisoners as he hurtled through the ages and all the major sciences, weighing up what was still to be done. Perhaps because it was his discipline, he was convinced that the next exciting scientific discoveries would be made not in physics but in biology. So, his Daedalus is not the familiar pioneer of flight but the first genetic engineer – the designer of the contraption that enabled King Minos's wife to mate with a bull and produce the Minotaur. Predictions have an unstable afterlife; their truth changes with the world, and while Haldane was brilliant on – and made a major contribution to – genetics, he was sceptical about the possibility of nuclear power. In the wake of the Second World War, and the realities of atom bombs, hydrogen bombs and nuclear power stations, his view of the sciences appeared wide of the mark. Later, when the Human Genome Project became news, he emerged as a prophet again. But while biotech certainly still preoccupies us two decades on, it is the computer that we see ushering in the definitive transformations of the age: artificial intelligence, machine learning, blockchain. And, remarkably, the computer is the one major modern development that not only Haldane but all the To-Day and To-Morrow writers missed.

By 1931, when the series was wound up, it ran to 110 books. They covered many of the subjects that mattered most at the time, from the future of marriage to the future of war, the future of art to the future of the British Empire. Most of To-Day and To-morrow's contributors were progressive, rationalist and intelligent, in favour of a World State and sceptical of eugenics. They wrote well, and were sometimes very funny, and the essays on the future of clothes and the future of nonsense in particular are wonderfully eccentric. And, of course, Haldane wasn't the only visionary. Many of the other writers contributed equally far-sighted ideas: Dora Russell suggested something akin to universal basic income for mothers; J. D. Bernal imagined wirelessly networked cyborgs – a cross between social media and the Internet of things; while Vera Brittain waxed confident about the enshrinement of women's rights in law.

What really stands out now is how, on the whole, the authors seemed to feel freer to be imaginative about the future than our contemporaries tend to be when they make predictions. There seems to be something about the long-form essay that freed the To-Day and To-morrow authors to see further ahead than a short journalistic piece could. Pursuing the logic of an individual vision, while also responding to what others projected, led them to dive deep into their topics in ways that are hard for the more tightly collaborative think-tank approaches of today to replicate. They were also more constructive than most of our contemporary future-thinkers. Of course we'd be mad not to worry about the climate crisis, the mass displacement of people(s), the risks of AI, new diseases (I'm writing this at the height – *maybe* – of COVID-19), asteroid collision and other apocalyptic scenarios. But if we're not only to survive these but also to thrive, we need to think beyond them as well as about them.

We are now almost a century on from the launch of To-Day and Tomorrow, and it feels like the right time to try this thought experiment again. So, for this first set of FUTURES, we have assembled a diverse group of brilliant writers with provocative ideas and visions. The point is not so much to prophesy as to generate new ideas about possibilities that could help us realise a future we might want to inhabit. To-Day and To-Morrow launched visions that helped create the modern world. The challenges we face now are, obviously, different from those of the 1920s and 30s. But our aspirations for FUTURES are the same. We want to change the conversation about what lies ahead so we can better imagine, understand and articulate the new worlds we might want to create.

Professor Max Saunders, March 2020

Max Saunders's Imagined Futures: Writing, Science, and Modernity in the To-Day and To-Morrow Book Series, 1923–31 *was published by Oxford University Press in 2019.*

Unbound is the world's first crowdfunding publisher, established in 2011.

We believe that wonderful things can happen when you clear a path for people who share a passion. That's why we've built a platform that brings together readers and authors to crowdfund books they believe in – and give fresh ideas that don't fit the traditional mould the chance they deserve.

This book is in your hands because readers made it possible. Everyone who pledged their support is listed below. Join them by visiting unbound.com and supporting a book today.

With special thanks to Jo Greenslade and Ark Schools

Caspar Addyman
Kathy Allen
John Attridge
William Ayles
Stuart Banks
David Barker
Stephen Beagrie
Ghassan Bejjani

Sarah Bennett
James Benussi
Steve Bindley
Kate Bird
Ian Blatchford
Su Bonfanti
Ed Bonnell
Stuart Bowdler

John Boxall
Zara Bredin
Catherine Breslin
Fabia Bromovsky
Victoria Bryant
Nicki Burns
Paul David Burns
Imogen Butler

Steve Byrne

Bob Callard

Ella Cape-Davenhill

NJ Cesar

Neil Chavner

Brendan Clarke

Nick Clarke

Peter Clasen

Jane Clifford

Fiona Clifft

Rhonda Cole

David-John Collins

Robert Collins

Alexander Colmer

Laura Colombino

Joseph Cordery

Andrew Correia

Peter Cosgrove

Nicola Crowell

Paolo Cuomo

Mary Curnock
Cook

Matthew d'Ancona

Tom Daly

Eileen Davidson

Joshua Davies

Edmund Davison

Victoria Davison

Sarah Denton

Jeremy Dicker

Lewis Dimmick

Kevin Donnellon

Linda Edge

Helen Edwards

Michael Elliott

Dominic Emery

Nic Fallows

Joanna Flood

Graham Folmer

Cedric Fontanille

Robert Forsyth

Oliver Francis

D Franklin

The FUTURES
team

Josh Gaillemin

Brian Gee

Lisa Gee

Sarah Gee

Charley Gilbert

Tom Gillingwater

Jordan Goble

George Goodfellow

John Gordon

Molly Gordon

Paul Gould

Brice Goureau

Melanie Gow

Keith Grady

Marlies Gration

Jon Gray

Scott Greenwell

Georgia Greer

John Grout

Steve Grycuk

Nicola Haggett

Greg Halfacre

Elizabeth Hall

Skye Hallam

Chloe Hardy

Nicola Harford

Richard Harvey

Nick Helweg-
Larsen

Paul Higgins

Gemma Hitchens

Maggie Hobbs

Meaghan Hook

Simon Howard

Nick Hubble

Simon Huggins

Jenny Hynd

Maggie Jack

Andy Johnson

Rebecca Jones

Danny Josephs

Tanu Kaskinen

Matthew Keegan

Christopher Kelly

Hilary Kemp

Luke Kemp

Fraser Kerr

Adam Khan

Dan Kieran

Andrew Knight

Christine Knight-
    Maunder

Lauren Knussen

Florian Kogler

Michael Kowalski

Simon Krystman

Nikki Land

Ben Lappin

Lyndsey Lawrence

Benedict Leigh

Fiona Lensvelt

Max Lensvelt

Sonny Leong

Miriam Levitin

Joanne Limburg

Linds

Valerie Lindsay

Ivan Lowe

Brian Lunn

Nicola Lynch

Rob MacAndrew

Andrew
    MacGarvey

Jem Mackay

Innes Macleod

Lewis MacRae

Paul Martin

Chris Matthias

Jenny McCullough

Michael McDowall

John McGowan

Neil McLaren

Adrian Melrose

John Mitchinson

Ronald Mitchinson

Kyna Morgan

Ian Morley

Tony Mulvahil

Robin Mulvihill

Peter Mummery

Tessa Murray

Janet Musgrove

James Nash

Carlo Navato

Kelvin Nel

John New

Sorcha Ní
    Mhaonaigh

Christopher Norris

Tim O'Connor

Mark O'Neill

Brian Padley

Michael Paley

Euan Palmer

Nic Parsons

Jaynesh Patel
Don Paterson
Sumit Paul-
    Choudhury
Matthew Pearson
Pauline Peirce
Nick Petre
Benjamin Poliak
Justin Pollard
Harriet Posner
Samantha Potter
Mark Poulson
Kate Pullinger
Slam Raman
Padraig Reade
Colette Reap
Suzanne Reynolds
John Rice Doyle
Stephen Ross
Charlotte Rump
Stuart Rutherford
Keith Ruttle
Cassedy Ryan
Ruth Sacks
Luke Sanders

Martin Saugnac
Max Saunders
Eleanor Scharer
Daniel
    Schwickerath
Duncan Scovil
Alexander Sehmer
Rossa Shanks
Gillian Shearn
Paul Skinner
Christopher Smith
Jan Smith
Katie Smith
Matthew Spicer
Paul Squires
Wendy Staden
Nicola Stanhope
Keith Stewart
Freddie Stockler
Nick Stringer
Elizabeth Suffling
Gilane Tawadros
Georgette Taylor
Richard Taylor
Bronwen Thomas

Luke Thornton
Lydia Titterington
Sophie Truepenny
Mark Turner
Geoff Underwood
Maarten van den
    Belt
Suzan Vanneck
Danielle Vides
Emma Visick
Gabriel Vogt
Claire Walker
Sir Harold Walker
Suzi Watford
Richard White
John Williams
Ross Williams
Catherine
    Williamson
Philip Wilson
Luke Young
Angelique &
    Stefano Zuppet